Dr. Faucet and the Case
of the Missing Drops

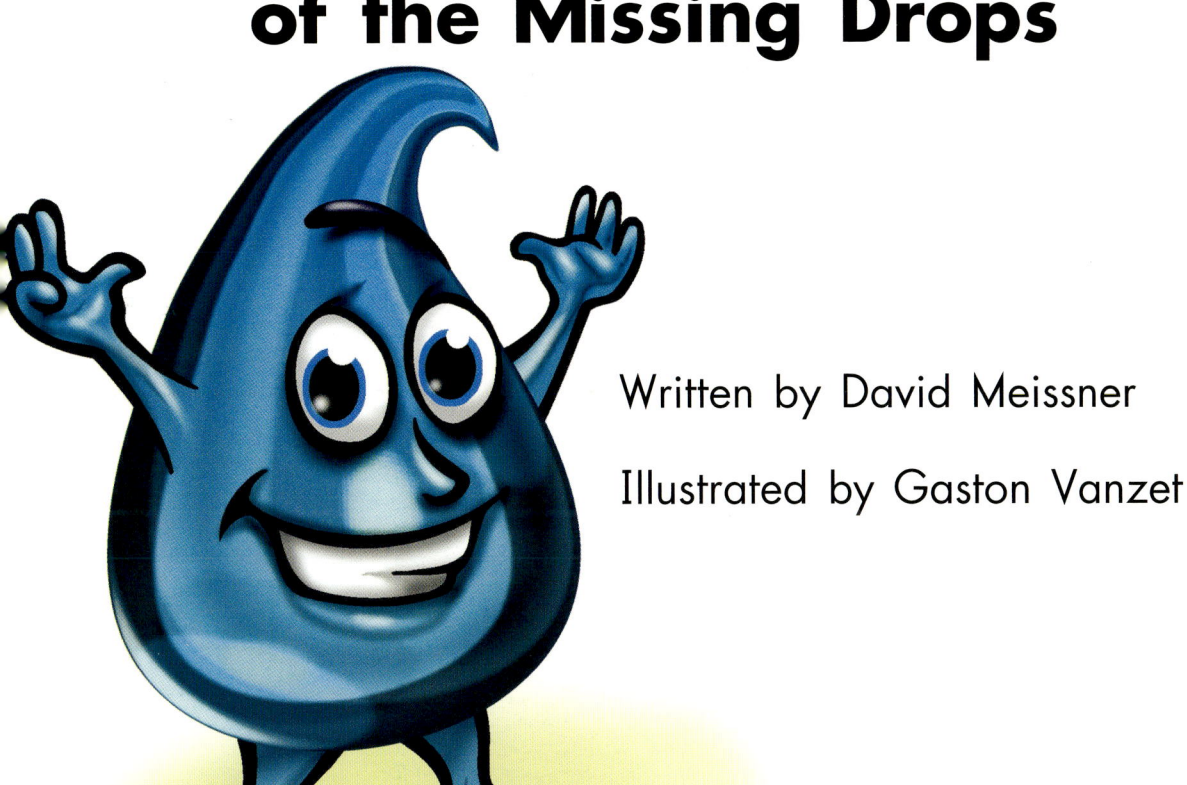

Written by David Meissner

Illustrated by Gaston Vanzet

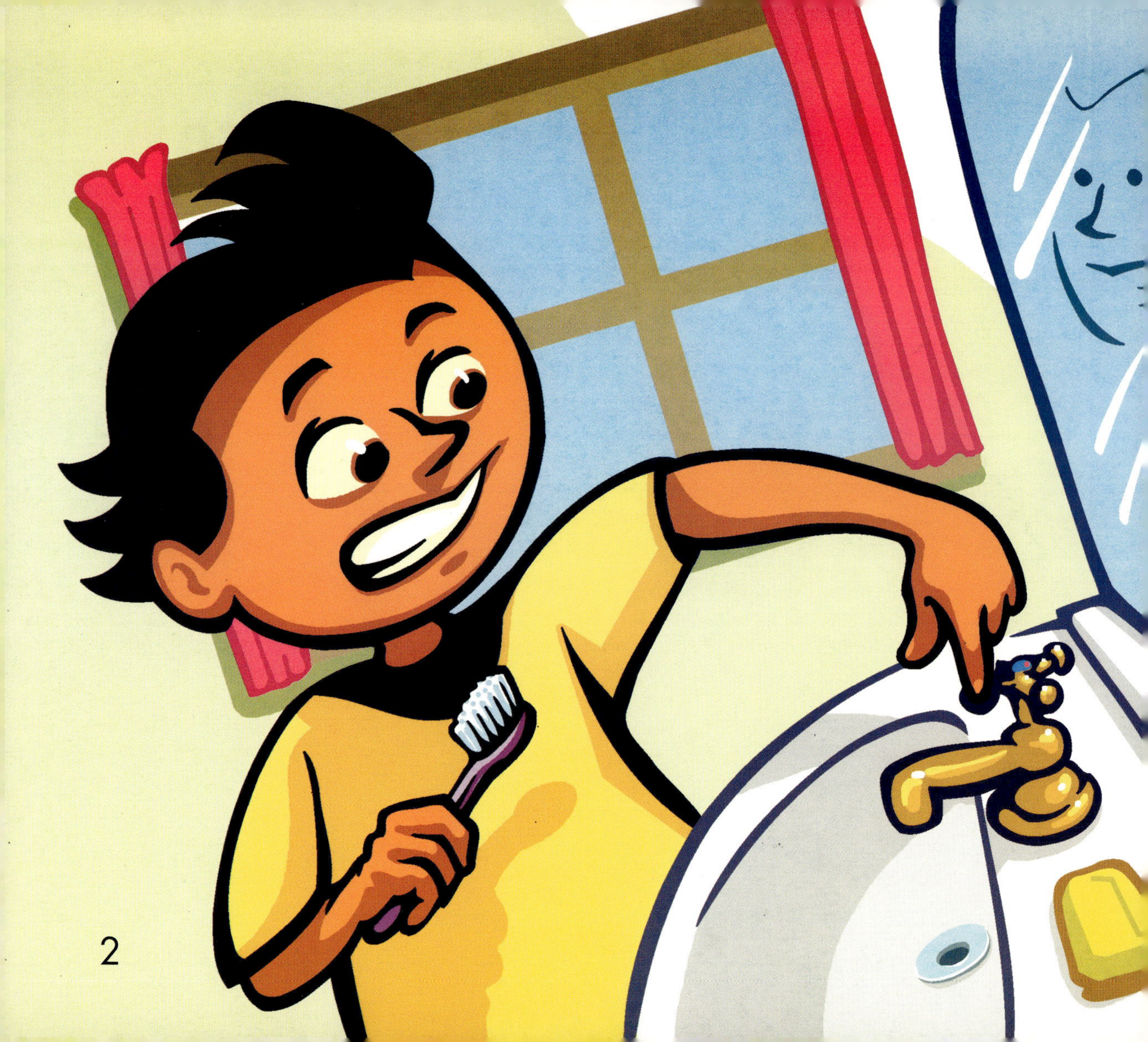

Once upon a time, a boy named Andy wanted to brush his teeth before school. But when he tried to turn on the faucet, no water came out. And when he looked in the toilet, it was empty too.

Andy's parents called Pipe-o-Rama to fix the problem. Within minutes, a plumber arrived at their house in a helicopter. His name was Dr. Faucet.

"Wow!" Andy exclaimed. "I didn't know plumbers flew helicopters!"

"I am a special kind of plumber," Dr. Faucet replied.

Dr. Faucet looked in the shower, in the sink, and in the toilet. He even peered inside the pipes. "This is very strange indeed," he said. "I cannot locate a single drop of water."

"But I need water to make coffee," said Andy's mom.

"And I need water to take a shower before work," said Andy's dad.

"I need water to brush my teeth!" Andy said.

All of the neighbors gathered around Dr. Faucet's helicopter. "We don't have any water either!" they shouted.

"Have no fear!" Dr. Faucet replied. "Dr. Faucet to the rescue! I'll be back soon."

Dr. Faucet climbed into his helicopter and flew off.

From up above, the city looked as dry as a desert. Every single swimming pool was empty. Even the rivers and lakes were dry.

"Now that is very odd," Dr. Faucet muttered to himself. "In all my years of plumbing, I have never seen anything quite like this."

Dr. Faucet knew that people were in trouble. They couldn't survive more than a few days without water.

Dr. Faucet steered his helicopter toward the coast. He was happy to see that the ocean was still full of water. But when he looked down at the beach, he couldn't believe his eyes.

Dr. Faucet landed his helicopter and walked along the beach for a closer look. Indeed, the beach was full of thousands of little water drops! They were having fun and relaxing under umbrellas. Some were even wearing sunglasses.

Dr. Faucet was friends with many water drops, but he had never seen them all go to the beach together. After a few minutes, Dr. Faucet recognized Slick the Water Drop.

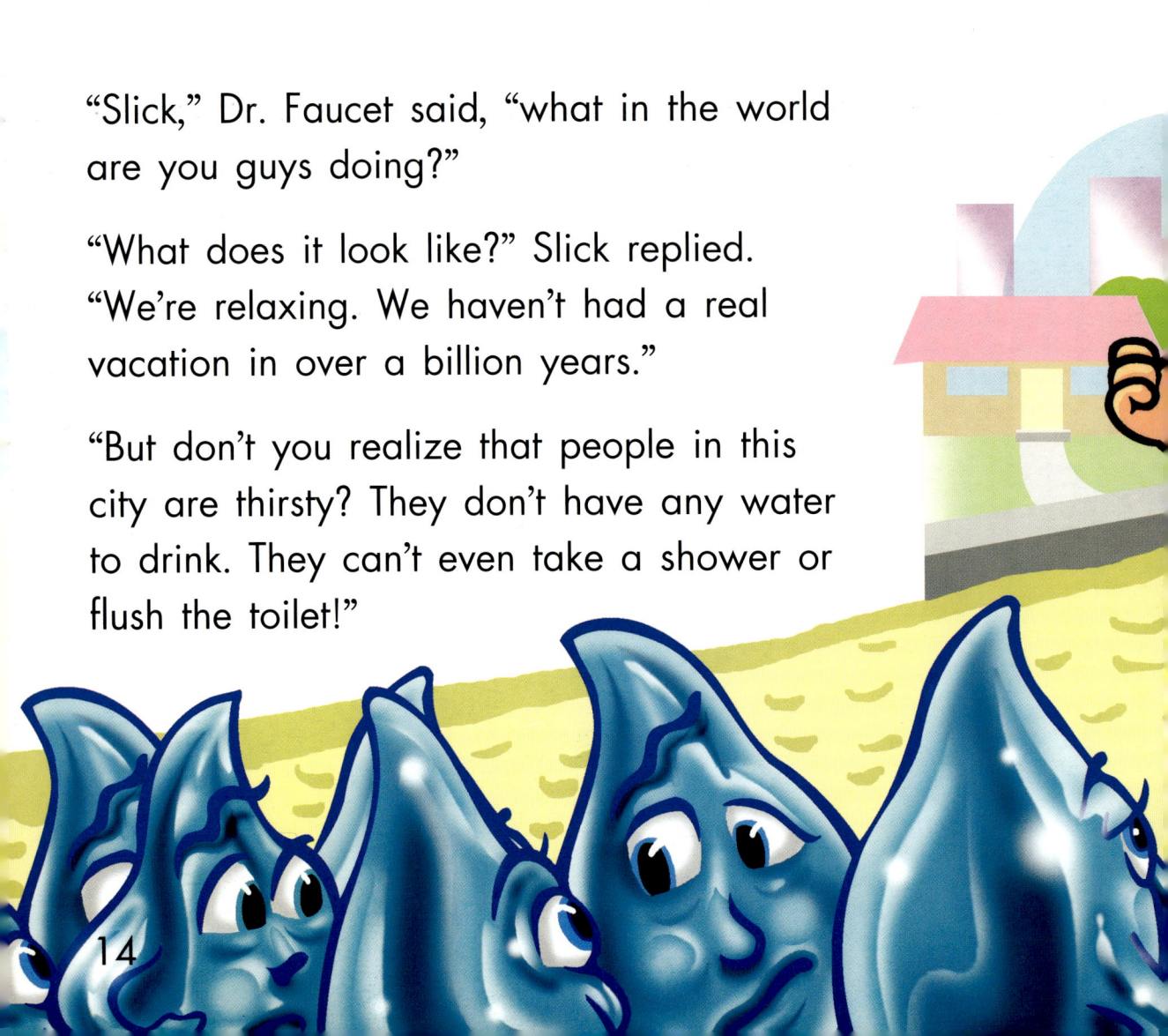

"Slick," Dr. Faucet said, "what in the world are you guys doing?"

"What does it look like?" Slick replied. "We're relaxing. We haven't had a real vacation in over a billion years."

"But don't you realize that people in this city are thirsty? They don't have any water to drink. They can't even take a shower or flush the toilet!"

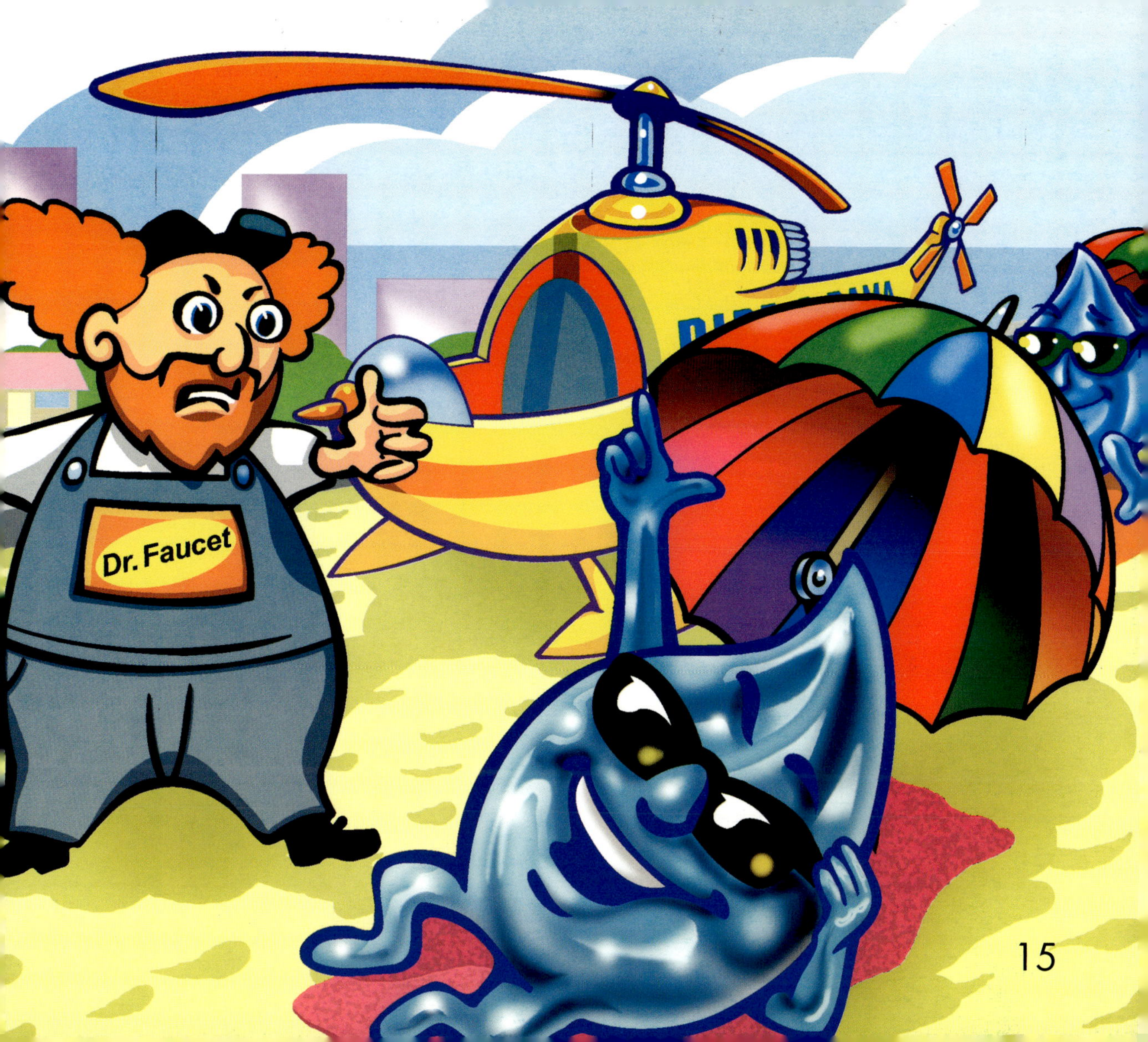
Dr. Faucet

"But Dr. Faucet, being water is hard work! Just last week I was flowing down a rushing river. I splashed onto a rock, and the sun evaporated me into thin air. Then yesterday I fell from a cloud and landed hard on the pavement of a city street. That's when I knew I needed a break."

"But I can't allow people, plants, and animals to die just because you want a vacation," Dr. Faucet replied. "Moving around the earth is part of your job."

Dr. Faucet walked back to his helicopter. He climbed in, revved up the engine, and buzzed close to the beach. "My apologies, Slick," he said. "I'm just doing my job."

The wind from the helicopter sent umbrellas flying everywhere. When the sun heated up the water drops, they evaporated high into the atmosphere.

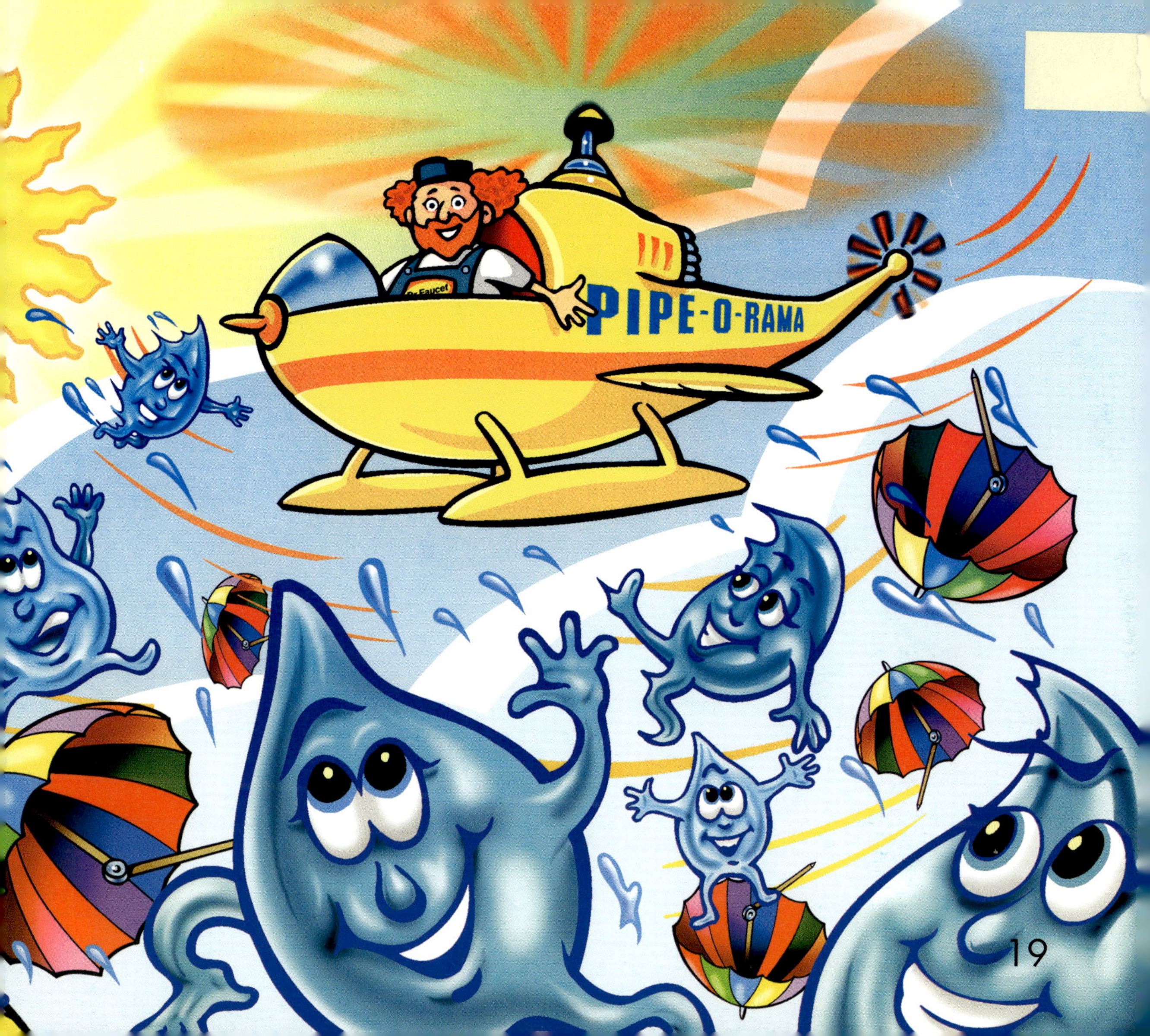
PIPE-O-RAMA

Soon large clouds formed over the city.
Then it started to rain, and rain, and rain.
Thousands of water drops fell from the sky.

When Dr. Faucet landed in front of Andy's house, all of the neighbors were cheering.

Dr. Faucet strolled into Andy's house and turned on the faucet. This time, water came rushing out.

Andy's mom served coffee. Andy's dad took a shower. And Andy's teeth looked as white as pearls.

"Wow!" Andy said. "You are a super plumber."

"I'm just trying to live up to my name," Dr. Faucet replied.